TABLE OF CONTENTS

Think about some of the ordinary things, living and nonliving, that make up your world—things like food, your yard, your pets, a pencil, jewelry, and snowflakes. Though different, they have something wonderful in common: crystals.

Crystals are solid substances in which **atoms** and **molecules** combine to create repeating **geometric** patterns such as triangles, squares, or rectangles. Crystals contain trillions—think millions times millions—of tiny regular shapes. The impurities within crystals give them their colors, which span the rainbow. Impurities are **elements** found in small amounts in the crystal. Iron can make quartz crystals appear yellow, while lead can make vanadinite appear red.

CRYSTALS, INSIDE AND OUT

Some gems, such as diamonds, are made of crystals. But crystals can sometimes play hide-and-seek, as with **geodes**. From the outside, geodes look like boring gray rocks. But when cracked or cut open, geodes reveal their true beauty in the crystals or gems—sometimes colored, sometimes clear—that line them.

ROCK-HARD FACT

Many, but not all, crystals contain **minerals**, hard materials found in nature that are **inorganic**—meaning they are not made of living things. Crystals, however, can be **organic**, as with sugar, which comes from plants.

Quartz
Inorganic

Sugar
Organic

Crystals are formed using just the right amounts of time, pressure, space, and heat. The way they form is called **crystallization**. Crystals occur when the molecules within a liquid form uniform geometric shapes as it cools. Crystals can also form when water **evaporates** from a solution, as when salt water dries up and leaves behind salt.

Some crystals—the ones made of minerals—find the perfect birthplace underground, where **magma** can slowly cool and crystallize. With time and pressure, the crystallized magma can even become beautiful gems.

GET TO KNOW YOUR CRYSTALS

Each crystal has its own unique blend of four characteristics: shape, color, transparency, and size. Try to identify the characteristics of the crystals in your kit.

SHAPE

The shapes of crystals—known as habits—come from the geometric patterns formed within them. Habits can be tree-like, square, in clusters, in cylinders, round, or a variety of other shapes.

COLOR

Crystals come in a rainbow of colors. The colors vary depending upon what elements are found within them.

TRANSPARENCY

Some crystals are **opaque**, meaning you can't see through them. Others appear cloudy, or **translucent**, allowing some light to pass through. Some are **transparent**, meaning you can see through them as you would a window.

SIZE

Crystals can be tiny or awe-inspiringly huge depending upon what they are made of and the amount of time, pressure, space, and heat they experience. (The crystals in your kit are small, but they're still a big deal!)

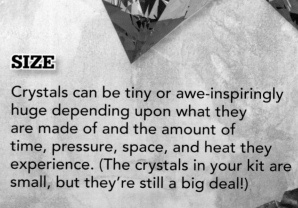

HOW DO CRYSTALS FORM?

MY CRYSTALS

SHAPE:

_____

☐ Round

☐ Square

☐ Tree-like

☐ Cluster

☐ Cylinder

Other (Describe)

_____

COLOR: (Describe)

_____

_____

TRANSPARENCY:

_____

☐ Transparent

☐ Translucent

☐ Opaque

ROCK-HARD FACT

What is something that grows even though it's not alive? A crystal! Crystals grow as more and more atoms are added to their structures. This can happen when melted rock cools or as liquid evaporates.

Geodes are like bland-looking Easter eggs of the rock world: They may look boring on the outside, but wait until you see what's inside. There you'll find glittering rings of colored crystals. But how did those crystals get inside the rock?

These hidden beauties have their beginnings in either **igneous** rock, where gas bubbles create holes, or voids, where crystals grow from minerals within the rock, or in **sedimentary** rock, where minerals fill cavities as time, pressure, space, and heat do their magic. As with other crystals, the colors come from impurities inside the rock.

ROCK-HARD FACT

Thunder eggs are a first cousin to geodes. From the outside, they look the same. Inside, they look almost the same. Both are filled with beautiful crystals and gems. But the difference is in the **cavity**: geodes have one, and thunder eggs do not.

A Real Rock Legend

In 1965, the residents of Oregon voted to name the thunder egg their state rock. According to legend, local Native Americans gave the much-loved rock their name because of fighting "thunder spirits" who would throw the rounded rocks on the ground.

DON'T JUDGE A
GEODE BY ITS COVER

MAKE YOUR OWN GEODES

Geodes can take many years to form—that is, unless you're making them yourself. Your geodes will actually form in much the same way as geodes in nature: the crystals from the salt will become solid as the water evaporates, and they will grow even larger than they were in the beginning.

Helping Hands

Be sure to recruit an adult helper (but you can still take all the credit for the results!).

WHAT YOU'LL NEED

- Eggshells, cracked as close to one end as possible and cleaned thoroughly with hot water (This is a good time to use your adult helper!)
- A pot of water
- Table salt, rock salt, or Epsom salt
- Ceramic coffee mugs or glass bowls
- A spoon
- Food coloring (Choose your favorites for your custom geodes!)
- An egg carton or a mini muffin tin
- Scissors
- Plate or pan

WHAT YOU'LL DO

1. Cut the eggshells in half lengthwise. Place the eggshells onto a plate or pan.

2. Bring the water to a boil.

3. Ask your helper to fill each coffee mug about halfway with the hot water.

4. Using the spoon, stir about half as much salt as water into the mug, adding the salt bit by bit as each addition dissolves.

5. Stir in the food coloring. You can add a different color to each mug or bowl.

6. Ask your helper to pour the hot liquid into the eggshells. Be careful not to overfill them.

7. Set the shells in a safe place. Crystals will form as the water evaporates.

Crystals, minerals, and gems have many similarities.

In fact, they can be the same thing—but not always. Let's take a look at what makes them alike and what makes them different.

CRYSTALS

- Have an orderly structure
- Are **three-dimensional**
- Have flat faces
- Have defined angles
- Can be organic or inorganic
- Need perfect conditions to grow

EXAMPLES:

Gold

Brown sugar

MINERALS

- Have an orderly structure
- Are formed naturally
- Are solid at room temperature
- Are always inorganic, except in the case of coal, which comes from plants
- Will contain crystals if allowed room to grow

EXAMPLES:

Dolomite

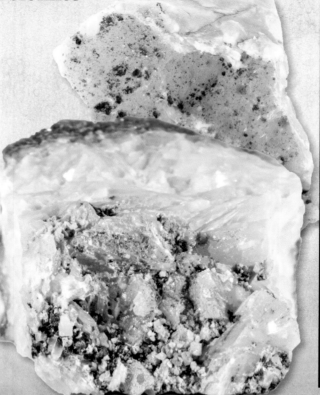

Crystal Systems

If you like minerals and gems, prepare to like geometry! Here are six geometric shapes of crystals.

CUBIC
Example: Halite

TETRAGONAL
Example: Zircon

HEXAGONAL
Example: Quartz

ORTHORHOMBIC
Example: Staurolite

MONOCLINIC
Example: Mica

TRICLINIC
Example: Cleavelandite

CRYSTAL, MINERAL,

GEMS

- Usually have a crystal structure
- Sometimes are crystals
- Usually are made of minerals
- Are usually, but not always, inorganic

EXAMPLES:

Labradorite
(inorganic)

Amber
(organic)

OR GEM?

ROCK-HARD FACT

Diamonds—classified as mineral, gem, and crystal—are considered the hardest natural material on Earth. They are made entirely of the element carbon and have many industrial uses, but they are most known as the world's most popular gemstone.

Because crystals only form under ideal conditions, you would think they would be rare. But you would be wrong. Our world contains a diverse array of crystals. Let's get to know a few of the more common ones.

CALCITE

Calcite is a crystal and a mineral found in limestone and marble, which can be used in construction.

FROST

The frost that forms on your windows in the winter can actually grow before your eyes and give you a good view of crystal structures.

PYRITE

If you ever think you've come across gold while digging, chances are good it's really pyrite, known as fool's gold. The iron within it gives it its gold color.

GOLD

Gold sometimes occurs in crystal form—as in the case of the single largest gold crystal ever found, valued at $1.5 million.

A GUIDE TO
COMMON CRYSTALS

SULFUR

If you've ever smelled water that had a serious funk, you can probably blame sulfur. Sulfur is also found in volcanoes and is used in rubber and insecticides.

HEMATITE

This iron-rich mineral contains steel-gray crystals and has a deep metallic shine. Because of the reddish color from the iron, it's sometimes used in paint or as a glass polish.

ROCK-HARD FACT

Crystals can be found, or not found, in surprising places. Some of the things you think are crystal—like your grandma's very breakable crystalware—are not crystal at all. But that aluminum folding chair you set up for picnics actually has a crystal structure.

Crystals are beautiful in their own right, but gemstones take the prize.

These spectacular crystals are cut according to the crystal shape within the gem to bring out its **brilliance**. The gem cutter must also cut around any defects found within the stone. It is a way to bring out the beauty and color of the gem without reducing its size—which usually is reduced by between 55 and 75 percent—more than needed.

Let's meet a few of the shining stars of the crystal world.

DIAMONDS

Diamonds are, by far, the most desired of all gemstones. Clear diamonds are the most famous, but colored ones—known as fancy diamonds—can be extremely valuable. The Hope Diamond is worth somewhere between $250 million and $350 million.

RHODOCHROSITE

Found in North and South America and Africa, this deep red and pink gem is thought by some to be the most beautiful crystal of them all. The famous football-sized specimen known as Alma King, found in Colorado, is considered the world's best example of rhodochrosite.

CITRINE

This rare type of quartz is the most popular of all yellow to orange stones, though it is also found in a brownish or reddish orange. It has often been confused with topaz.

Rhodochrosite

Hope Diamond

BEAUTIFUL CRYSTALS:
GEMSTONES

CAT'S EYE QUARTZ

Imperfections within the quartz give this gem its famous slitted cat's eye effect, known as chatoyancy. Usually gray in color, the gem can be found in other colors, such as green, for a more realistic cat's eye effect.

ROSE QUARTZ

What this soft to medium pink gem lacks in transparency, it more than makes up for in size. This commonly found crystal often grows very large, allowing large gemstones to be cut from it.

ROCK-HARD FACT

The minerals within crystals give them their beautiful colors. Pure quartz, for instance, has no color, but when you add iron, you can have an amethyst. **Radiation** can produce smoky quartz, while the green mineral chlorite causes quartz to turn green.

Smoky quartz

Amethyst

Green quartz

Making the Cut

Fewer than 100 of the more than 4,000 minerals found on Earth are worthy to be called gems. Because of their rareness and value, they once belonged almost exclusively to royalty.

AVENTURINE

This green quartz sparkles because of flecks of impurities within it. Its extra sparkle helps it score points as a gemstone. Though most often green, aventurine can also be found in orange, yellow, red, pink, brown, white, gray, and blue.

13

SO WHAT COLOR IS FLUORITE REALLY?

Fluorite is considered a purple crystal. But fluorite, which can appear almost any color depending upon the light and angle at which it's viewed, likes to keep people guessing. Light reacts with the chemicals and the crystal structure within the fluorite to create this effect. Sometimes fluorite can even appear to have bands of color. This is the result of the heat and pressure the crystal experiences while forming in sedimentary rock layers.

THE STONE THAT GUIDED VIKINGS

Long before the invention of compasses, 10th-century Vikings wrote of a mysterious "sunstone" they used to locate the sun as they navigated their ships on cloudy days. Ten centuries later, scientists say they have solved the mystery of the sunstone. They believe Vikings used a calcite crystal, also known as Icelandic spar. Looking through Icelandic spar will give you double vision—unless you line it up at a right angle to a light. Then instead of a double image, you see a single point that would allow you to determine the position of the sun. A study shows these "sunstones" helped the Vikings navigate 1,600 miles (2,575 km) of ocean from Greenland to Norway.

QUARTZ: YOUR NEW MAIN SQUEEZE

When you squeeze a plastic bottle, something comes out of it. We expect that. We don't expect something to come out of a quartz crystal when we squeeze it, but it does. When you squeeze quartz, it releases an electrical charge. That charge builds up with more pressure. This is called the **piezoelectric effect**. This effect turns quartz into a type of battery as the crystal vibrates in a precise and constant way, making it perfect for use in watches and electronics. So if your watch keeps perfect time, you can probably thank a quartz!

STRANGE-BUT-TRUE STORIES:
QUIRKY CRYSTALS

AWESOME AUTUNITE

Under normal light, autunite is yellow to green. But when you shine an ultraviolet light upon it, it glows a spooky green. And here's something even spookier: it glows because it's **radioactive!** Autunite contains the element uranium, which can be used to make power and bombs. Its glowing effect makes it **fluorescent**. When the ultraviolet light is turned off, autunite goes back to its normal color.

ROCK-HARD FACT

Earth's core was once thought to be one giant crystal. Scientists have found, however, that it's likely a mass of many smaller crystals. Either way, Earth is crystal to the core.

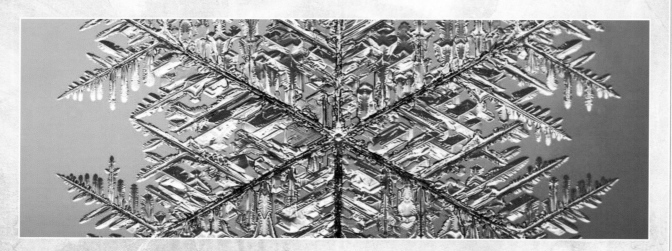

Every winter as you watch those first few snowflakes fall from the sky, you may not be able to help thinking of them as magical. But the magic of snowflakes—which would more correctly be called snow crystals—is 100 percent science.

Every snowflake has six sides and contains about 200 crystals. Its shape is determined by the temperature and the humidity, or amount of moisture in the air, when it's formed. It experiences changes in temperature and humidity as it falls through the clouds. Because no two snowflakes follow the exact same path—meaning they don't experience identical conditions—it's believed no two are exactly alike.

Snowflakes have a **symmetrical** design, meaning that their arms would line up with each other if you were to fold them in half. But you will find slight differences in the points along each arm, meaning they're also **asymmetrical**.

Dust or pollen particles are the "seeds" from which snowflakes grow as they get covered in moisture high up in the sky, resulting in ice crystals. Developing their distinct hexagonal shape, snowflakes then grow as they're exposed to more moisture and cold. The farther they fall, the more they grow.

Don't Eat the White Snow

We've all heard about not eating the yellow snow, but now you can add white snow to the list. So what's so bad about white snow? It may look clean, but it actually collects pollutants—bad-for-you stuff like mercury and soot from the air—that you can't see.

NATURE'S COOLEST

STELLAR DENDRITES

TRIANGULAR CRYSTALS

COLUMNS AND NEEDLES

TWELVE-BRANCHED SNOWFLAKES

CAPPED COLUMNS

FERNLIKE STELLAR DENDRITES

DIAMOND DUST CRYSTALS

RIMED SNOWFLAKES AND GRAUPEL

ARTWORK

ROCK-HARD FACT

The smallest snowflakes, called diamond dust crystals, can be as small as the width of a human hair and are found in the coldest places on Earth. The biggest one ever photographed was .4 in (10 mm) wide—small compared with many things but huge for a snowflake!

You sprinkle salt on your French fries and spoon sugar on your cereal.

Why? Well, everyone knows salt and sugar help make food delicious. And here's a tasty tidbit: Salt and sugar are crystals. In fact, crystals are responsible for the texture, shelf life, mouth feel, and quality of many of our favorite foods.

You can find crystals in chewing gum, butter, margarine, and ice cream.
In fact, ice cream is often a combination of three types of crystals: ice crystals, fat crystals, and crystals from the sugar found in milk. Sometimes crystals are fully formed in foods, and sometimes they're only partly formed. How well formed they are and what size they are gives food the right texture and mouth feel.
You can purify sugars and fats using crystallization, and the results can be purely delicious.

Salt crystals

THE CRYSTALS WE EAT

For ice cream or homemade fudge to taste its best, the crystals within them must be small. That's one reason constant stirring is so important. Food manufacturers have learned that the size, shape, and amount of crystals within food greatly affect food quality and its shelf life (the amount of time it can safely be stored). They carefully watch what type of ice crystals form on food during chilling to preserve food quality.

Sugar crystals

ROCK-HARD FACT

Crystals make chocolate one of the most loved foods in the world. Chocolate has to be prepared just right to develop the tight crystal structure that gives it that smooth, creamy mouth feel so many of us crave—and yes, that causes us to lick our fingers.

Our world is full of crystals so that you can't avoid them even if you wanted to. But there are a few you may want to avoid, and a few more you may want to give a closer look. Welcome to the world of weird!

CHANGER

Every day, the sun comes up, creating light. Each evening, the sun goes down, creating darkness. The same thing happens with hackmanite. Hackmanite turns a pale blue, white, or gray within seconds of being exposed to daylight and slowly returns to a deep purple in the dark. The effect is similar to what happens with glasses that become sunglasses in outdoor light. Sometimes used as a gem, hackmanite will do its color-changing trick over and over again unless it is heated. Then the show is over.

DANGER

Most crystals are beautiful. But with some, there's more than meets the eye. Arsenopyrite contains arsenic, a deadly poison that is the stuff of murder mysteries. (That's why people shout at the screen telling actors not to drink what their enemies have just given them!) Torbernite is a lovely green crystal with a pearly glow. If you found one, it probably would become a treasured part of your rock collection—if it didn't contain radioactive uranium, that is.

THE WORLD'S WEIRDEST CRYSTALS

AND STRANGER STILL

With its transparent deep red color and glittery appearance from the silver within it, you may have a hard time looking away from proustite. But you would have to, because this delicate crystal has to be stored in the dark. Prolonged exposure to light turns the stone cloudy and black. Sometimes the blackening occurs only on the surface and can be washed away, but sometimes it destroys the beautiful red stone forever. Here's another dark side to proustite: like arsenopyrite, it contains arsenic.

TUNE IN FOR MORE

It's fair to say that galena has changed the world. In the early 1900s, scientists found the mineral-rich crystal could pull voices and music out of radio waves. It can also conduct electricity. The crystal radio was born. Using galena, radio waves can be converted into an electrical signal and then into sound heard through speakers. Radios changed the world by giving people quick access to news and entertainment.

21

Crystals often wow us with their complex structures and beauty.

Let's take a closer look at some common crystals as seen under a microscope.

A CRYSTAL FOREST

You typically wouldn't think of ammonium chloride— used to coat metals and in medicine—as beautiful. But you would quickly change your mind once you looked at it under a microscope, where it looks like a forest growing before your eyes.

THE COLORS YOU DON'T SEE

Creamy, white coconut butter is a common kitchen staple. So it would surprise you to see the bright blue and deep green crystals within it. If you don't like blue or green food, tell your mom you can't eat coconut butter!

SAND AS YOU'VE NEVER SEEN IT

If you were to draw a sandy beach, you would probably reach for your tan crayon or marker. But **microscopic** views of sand may make you rethink that choice. Within the tiny fragments of broken, worn rock are a rainbow of colorful crystals, fragments of shells, and pieces of volcanic rock. In Sri Lanka in Asia, sand can even contain fragments of rubies, a precious gem. Sand, it seems, is anything but bland.

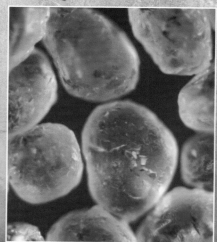

TINY CRYSTALS

MIND-BLOWING METAL

A close-up look at metals silver and lead may be worth its weight in gold. Objects made of these metals are heavy and strong. But the metals have their beginnings in delicate, branching, frostlike crystals that create magical, seldom-seen worlds.

ROCK-HARD FACT

Chalcedony, a type of quartz that is considered a semiprecious (or lesser) gem, contains crystals so tiny that they can't be seen without a microscope. The closer you look at chalcedony, the more beautiful it becomes.

We've talked about how crystals will continue to grow given the right combination of time, pressure, space, and heat. These crystals are proof! If you love crystals, then these giants will give you a whole lot to love.

WELCOME TO THE ICE AGE

The Crystal Cave in Bermuda was formed during the Ice Age but wasn't discovered until 1905, when a boy playing cricket with his friend noticed warm air coming from a crack in the ground near where the ball landed. Soon a 14-year-old carrying a bicycle lamp was lowered into this stunning cave, becoming the first person to see it. Author Mark Twain later visited and described "shining stalactites, thousands and thousands of them as white as sugar, and thousands and thousands brown and pink and other tints."

WE'RE TALKING REALLY BIG

Cave of the Crystals in Chihuahua, Mexico, is home of the world's largest crystals, measuring 36 ft. (11 m) long, 4 ft. (1.2 m) wide, and weighing about 55 tons (50 tonnes) each. The crystals formed when the cave filled with water, and the magma beneath the cave slowly cooked the gypsum minerals in the water to create giant columns of the selenite minerals. The crystals are done growing— that is, unless the cave floods again.

PREPARE TO BE ENCHANTED

A giant geode and an equally giant amethyst have found a home in a so-called enchanted cave in Australia's Crystal Castle attraction. The geode is filled with smoky quartz, a cousin of the amethyst. People visit the cave to experience the stones' "healing energies." Members of royalty, Hollywood actors, and famous musicians have been among the visitors.

NOT-SO-TINY CRYSTALS

THIS WON'T FIT IN A WATCH

Quartz is commonly used in watches and electronics, but not this monster. At 30,865 lb. (14,000 kg), it is considered the world's largest quartz cluster. It was discovered in 1985 at the bottom of a deep cave beneath a mine and took three years to **excavate**. It is now on display in a museum in Namibia, Africa.

ROCK-HARD FACT

Many geodes are small enough to fit into your hand—but not this one. Crystal Cave in Put-in-Bay, Ohio, is the world's largest geode. Workers discovered the cave in 1897 while digging a well for the winery above it. Many of the blue crystals were harvested to use in fireworks before the cave became a tourist attraction.

WHAT CAME FIRST: THE GEODE OR THE TOAD?

When you open a geode, it's enough of a surprise to find beautiful crystals inside. But instead of finding something spiky, imagine finding something slimy. People have reported finding living frogs or toads inside geodes. Usually the animal will come to life for a few minutes and then will turn a sickly gray and die.

Scientists have a couple of theories about how the animals get there and how they survive. After all, **geologists** believe it could take thousands of years for a geode to form. One **theory** is that the geode forms around a frog or toad egg that later hatched inside the rock. Some people say the rock could have formed around the animal while it was in a dormant state in which its breathing, heart rate, and other bodily functions had slowed down. Protection from air and light could extend the life of the animal, allowing it to live a really, really long time—until finally someone opens its airtight home.

STRANGE-BUT-TRUE STORIES:
CRYSTAL TOMBS

WHEN METAL MEETS ROCK

When we say crystals can contain metals, and metals can contain crystals, we didn't quite have these metals in mind. Some people have reported finding strange metal objects inside geodes: spark plugs, a modern bullet, and other strange manmade and even elaborate metal objects. How did modern objects find their way inside rocks that are supposed to take thousands of years to form? Are the objects proof that aliens once lived on our planet? Or are scientists wrong about how long it takes for geodes to form? Time—and science—will tell.

ROCK-HARD FACT

Most geodes are found in the Americas, with the largest number found in the United States. The more likely you are to find a geode, the more likely you are to find something breathtaking (literally, as in the case of our frogs and toads) inside it.

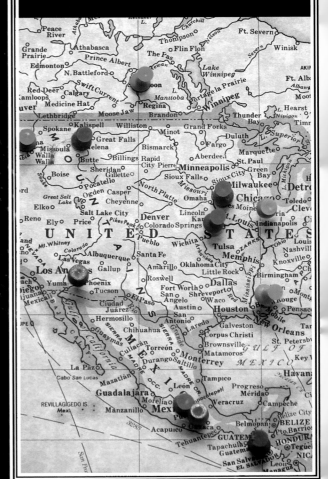

The world you live in looks very different from the world your grandparents or great-grandparents knew. It even looks different from the one your parents knew as kids. That's because of advances in **technology**, and crystals get at least part of the credit.

We've learned about how crystals have been used in radios and watches. But their usefulness in technology goes beyond those common gadgets.

Their ability to produce and conduct electricity and vibrate in a steady, constant way (the piezoelectric effect we learned about on pp. 14-15) makes them useful in smartphones, digital cameras, TVs, computers, and receivers.

CRYSTALS IN
TECHNOLOGY

As pollution from vehicle **emissions** continues to affect our air quality, researchers in California are looking at ways to use crystals to generate power for cars. Crystals could create a renewable energy source—one that won't run out—without creating air pollution.

Scientists are also studying crystallization, which is used to purify chemicals as they're being made, in an effort to find better ways to make medicines.

ROCK-HARD FACT

Scientists have come up with a way to preserve important documents for billions of years using crystals. Each small disc can hold as much information as more than 20,000 smartphones. Lasers **encode** information into structures too tiny to see with the naked eye onto tiny pieces of quartz. The structures change the way light travels through the glass around the quartz, and the data can then be read by special devices.

We've all seen crabs, lobsters, and clams at a beach or aquarium or on TV. But did you ever stop to think about how they got their shells? These amazing creatures produce their own shells made of microscopic crystals using a process known as **biomineralization**.

Biomineralization allows animals to create their own protection against **predators**. If you've ever been unlucky enough to get a sea urchin spine in your foot, you've experienced that creature's defense system thanks to biomineralization.

Biomineralization can be beautiful as well as useful. Some sea creatures create coral, an external skeleton made of crystals. Pearls, grown inside oysters, are made of crystals, as are bird and mammal skeletons.

Scientists recently found a type of crystal made from living **bacteria**. Researchers made the discovery while looking at bacteria on a glass slide under a microscope. As the tiny creatures spun around, they bunched together into a

crystal structure. The bacteria did this to get enough food so they could continue to grow.

CRYSTALLIZED CRITTERS

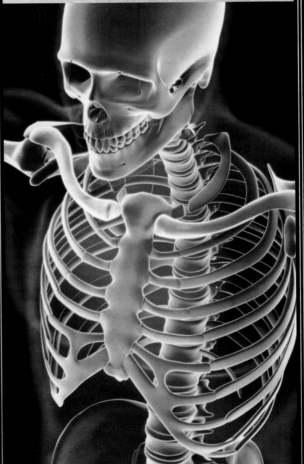

ROCK-HARD FACT

Your body is a walking example of biomineralization. Your skeleton is made of crystals. You are able to balance because of crystals in your ear. You can chew your food because of the crystals within your teeth. Weirder yet, crystals in your brain generate electricity!

We've learned about crystals with strange and almost magical powers.

Now get ready to learn about some crystals that are truly out of this world!

ALIEN GEMS

Some meteorites, like pallasite, are pretty enough to be used as gems. One such gem, pallasite peridot, is one of the most rare gems on Earth. Sometimes asteroids and meteorites cause the formation of gems. That's what happened with moldavite, which formed long ago when an asteroid fell in Europe. Is it by chance that moldavite is an alien green? You decide.

BLUE SALT CRYSTALS

In 1998, two meteorites that became named Zag and Monahans fell to Earth. Years later, scientists had the technology to test them. When they did, what they found was amazing: the meteorites contained blue salt crystals that look like blue sapphire gemstones, and within the crystals were organic matter including the building blocks of life. Scientists think the salt crystals came from an asteroid belt named Ceres, which they believe could harbor life.

CRYSTALS FROM SPACE

QUASICRYSTALS

Researchers identified a strange rule-breaking crystal called a quasicrystal (KWAHZ-eye-kristul) in 1982. So what's weird about quasicrystals? They follow some of the rules of crystals, but their atoms are arranged in patterns that don't repeat themselves. "There can be no such creature," one scientist said in amazement while studying them. Until 2007, they were made in labs. But then another researcher found one in a museum rock collection. The sample came from a meteorite found in Russia. No wonder quasicrystals break the rules: they're aliens!

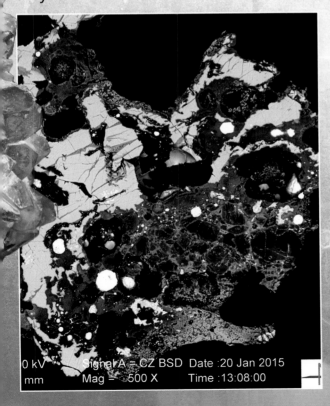

SPACE DIAMONDS

In 2008, a meteorite fell in Sudan. The scientists who studied it found something very unexpected with it: space diamonds! They believe the diamonds are part of a lost planet that once was found between Mercury and Mars. Inside the diamonds they found substances that had only been found on Earth to that point. The diamonds came from a type of meteorite that often contains clusters of diamonds.

1 mm

ROCK-HARD FACT

Libyan desert glass, believed to have been made from sand that melted during a meteorite impact, has always had such great value that it was used as the center stone of a pendant buried with King Tut. The alien-made glass is only found at the border of Egypt and Libya.

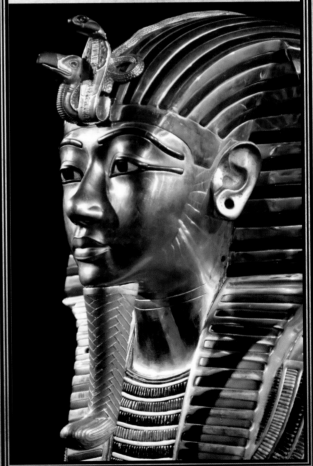

Many crystals are mined and then sold. Arkansas, Colorado, and Brazil are known for their quartz mines. Workers dig underground to unearth specimens. Their work is dangerous and time consuming, but the results—which sometimes can include gold-crusted quartz— are well worth the effort.

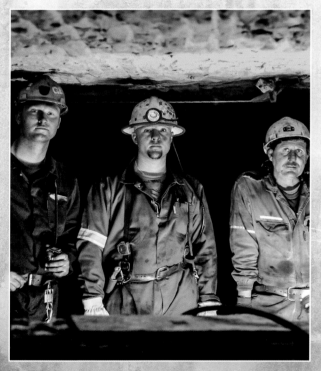

Always remember to wear old clothes and take plenty of water, sunscreen, and a first-aid kit if you go on a dig for crystals.

Some mines around Mount Ida, Ark., considered the quartz capital of the world, have areas open to the public. Visitors can bring garden tools, a screwdriver, and a bucket and can walk away with a good collection of quartz.

MINE, MINE, AND YOURS:
UNEARTHING CRYSTALS

If you prefer a little color to your quartz, you can look for your own amethysts during public dig days in Northern Georgia. The crystals are often found in clumps of dark red or white clay. Sometimes amethysts hide inside rock.

Another great place to look for crystals is around fault zones, where you can find ribbons of quartz or even gold that come to the surface during earthquakes.

Natural hot springs are also good places to look for crystals. The heat helps form crystals, which sometimes are pushed to the surface. The same is true of areas like the Cascade Mountains in Washington and Northern California, where crystals result from volcanoes.

ROCK-HARD FACT

Amber and coral, though they are organic and have no crystal structure, are considered gemstones. Amber is formed from the resin of trees, and pearls are formed as oysters secrete a coating over irritants within them.

AND GEODES

Crystals have changed our world—and our universe— and they continue to be a source of amazement to scientists. So how can they be any more amazing? Well, you're about to find out!

THE WORLD'S MOST VALUABLE CRYSTAL

Diamonds are the most beloved of all crystals, and the diamond known as the Pink Star outshines them all. In 2017, the giant diamond sold for $71 million, breaking the record for the highest price ever paid on a gemstone.

CRYSTALLIZED DNA

Scientists have known that almost any solid can crystallize. But they were surprised to see that DNA, a type of blueprint carried in our cells, will crystallize in liquid. Just as each person is unique, each DNA strand creates unique and beautiful crystal patterns. "The huge range of crystal structure is amazing," one scientist said. Researchers are looking for ways to use what they have learned from crystallized DNA in technology and medicine.

CRYSTAL COMETS

When you look up into the night sky and see a comet's tail of dust and ice, you may be looking at crystals that formed at the edge of our solar system. Scientists say the flares from the sun helps form crystals from minerals within a comet's icy tail.

AMAZING FACTS
ABOUT CRYSTALS

CRYSTAL WALLS

Gypsum is a soft mineral often found as a crystal in sedimentary rock layers. Chances are excellent you're surrounded by it right now and you don't even know it. That's because gypsum is used to make the drywall and plaster found within your walls. So maybe you should call your house a crystal palace!

HEALING CRYSTALS

Some people believe crystals have special powers. Citrine, they say, helps your dreams come true, and amethyst is said to relieve stress. To be more creative, people recommend carnelian, while black tourmaline is rumored to help you break bad habits.

ROCK-HARD FACT

Stalagmites and stalactites form as water containing mineral deposits drips slowly over many years. Stalactites hang from cave ceilings, and stalagmites shoot up from cave floors. (To remember which is which, think "g" for ground and "c" for ceiling.) Adding to their cool factor is the fact they're made of, and sometimes even covered with, crystals.

Crystals have left an imprint on many cultures throughout history. People believed crystals gave them special powers or protection—a belief that continues among some today.

SEEKING CLEAR ANSWERS

The Japanese would gaze into balls made of clear quartz to get answers to questions or to foretell the future. Some people still rely upon crystal balls today. Psychic Jeane Dixon used a crystal ball to predict that a man named Nikolai Bulganin would become a leader of the Soviet Union. Two years later, Dixon's prediction came true—or was it just a coincidence?

PROTECTION IN BATTLE

Before going into battle, Greek soldiers would rub crushed hematite onto their bodies because they believed it would help them defeat their enemies. They also believed clear quartz was a type of ice that fell from heaven. Like the Greeks, Romans also used crystals for protection in battle. They also believed crystals promoted good health and brought good fortune.

A SYMBOL AND SOURCE OF WEALTH

In Ancient Rome, the wealthy covered their windows with a type of gypsum that forms sheets of crystals. One emperor named Tiberius made an entire greenhouse using hundreds of sheets of clear gypsum. The Romans made a lot of money mining and selling the mineral, so maybe crystals brought them good fortune after all.

CRYSTALS THROUGHOUT

ANCIENT MEDICINE

The Chinese have used crystals in acupuncture—an ancient medicine that uses needles that prick the skin to bring healing—for thousands of years. They believe certain crystals can heal specific illnesses. Clear quartz is considered a "master healer," while citrine is used for digestive problems. Green aventurine is believed to cure headaches.

HELP IN THE AFTERLIFE

Ancient Egyptians would place quartz upon the foreheads of their dead to help guide them in the afterlife. Their priests would carry containers of quartz to balance competing energies within them.

HISTORY

THE LOST CRYSTAL CITY

Mount Shasta in Northern California is a popular vacation spot. Some visitors never leave, saying they're drawn by the mountain's energy. But what's even more strange is the story behind—or rather, inside—the mountain. According to legend, inside the mountain is the lost crystal city of Telos. The people who lived in Telos went to war with the people of the lost city of Atlantis, according to the story.

The war was so violent that it sank the land beneath both people.

The people of Telos went to live inside the mountain and remain there today—well, mostly. About 80 years ago, locals say, some very tall people dressed in robes came into town to do some shopping and paid in gold. Locals also believe the saucer-shaped clouds that sometimes form over the mountain hide alien ships that bring supplies to the hidden crystal city within.

STRANGE-BUT-TRUE STORIES:
THE STUFF OF LEGENDS

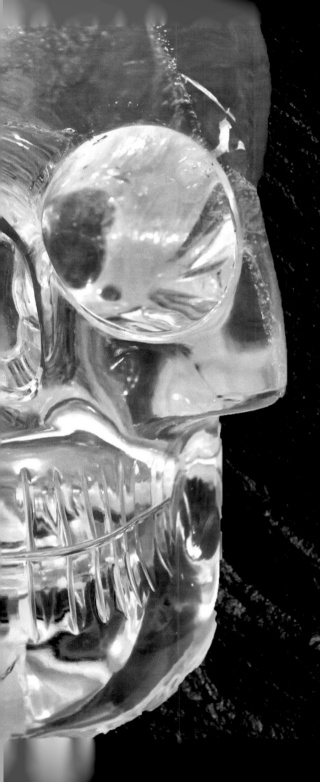

CRYSTAL SKULLS!

Maybe the city of Telos is too weird to be real, but crystal skulls are too weird and too real. About 12 of these carved quartz skulls can be found around the world. Experts believe they come from Mexico or somewhere in Central America.

But some people have other theories: The skulls were made by people from Atlantis (before the people of Telos sent them to their doom, we can assume), or the skulls were carved by aliens. Their strange ideas are meant to explain the skulls' strange powers—the power to kill, the power to heal, mental powers, and power over death. Some even say the skulls are a type of computer. But experts at the British Museum and the Smithsonian Institution now say they can see marks of modern tools on the skulls that would date them to the mid- to late 1800s. Maybe the skulls aren't so mysterious after all.

ROCK-HARD FACT

According to Greek legend, amethyst got its purple color as the Greek god Dionysus cried tears of wine over a beautiful young woman named Amethyst, who had been turned into a quartz statue.

When most people define a crystal, they say it is always a solid. But the truth is a little more fluid than that. Liquid crystals are somewhere between a liquid and a solid. They are usually liquid, but the molecules within them move around like crystals. But like water, liquid crystals can become a solid or a gas.

The order of liquid crystals can be changed with magnetic, electrical, and other forces. They are also sensitive to temperature. Cold makes the crystals turn solid, and heat makes them turn liquid. Often they're somewhere in between.

SOLID FACTS ON LIQUID CRYSTAL

We now know liquid crystals are found in snail slime, the wings of insects, and some stars. Today, they're used in making lipsticks, strong plastics, and laundry detergent, among other products. But their most popular use is in liquid-crystal displays, or LCDs.

LCDs are used in many items that use screens: calculators, TVs, thermometers, clocks, computers, cellphones, and digital watches, to name a few. LCD technology has allowed TVs to become thinner, lighter, and more energy-efficient.

Liquid crystal technology is still young, and researchers are still studying ways to use it. Scientists are looking at creating supercomputers and superconductors, which conduct energy super-fast without overheating, using a special kind of three-dimensional liquid crystal.

ROCK-HARD FACT

Liquid crystal technology has its beginnings in the carrot. In the late 19th century, an Austrian scientist was studying compounds within carrots when he discovered one compound was in liquid crystal form, making it useful in creating and changing images. It wasn't until many years later that liquid crystals were used in that way, however.

Crystals and geodes have centuries of stories to tell if we take the time to study them. Some people spend their lives studying them, but many of their mysteries remain unsolved. Let's meet some experts.

GEOLOGIST

Geologists study materials within the earth and the history they reveal. They are experts in rocks and rock formation, and they study geologic events such as landslides, volcanoes, floods, and earthquakes.

SO YOU WANT TO
BE AN EXPERT

CRYSTALLOGRAPHER

If you have an eye for detail and you love science, crystallography could be in your future. Crystallographers study crystals at the atomic level, and they have to be experts in many areas of science. They look at organic and inorganic crystals—everything from gemstones to viruses.

GEMOLOGIST

Gemologists love things shiny and pretty, but they also love science. As experts in geology who study gemstones, they learn how gemstones are created, study their properties, and give them grades for their quality.

LAPIDARY

A **lapidary** cuts and polishes gemstones. To do this, lapidaries must have very steady hands, a broad knowledge of gemstones, and a lot of creativity that allows them to look at gemstones and envision how to make them look their very best so they can be used in jewelry.

MINERALOLOGIST

Crystals and minerals are often one and the same. Mineralogists study the chemical and crystal structures of minerals. Sometimes they work for mining companies so they can collect, prepare, and test samples.

ASYMMETRICAL

having parts that don't line up with each other

ATOM

the smallest unit of matter

BACTERIA

a single-cell creature that can be seen using a microscope

BIOMINERALIZATION

the process through which living things produce minerals

BRILLIANCE

the ability to reflect light to bring out color

CAVITY

a hole or space inside something

CRYSTAL

a solid substance in which atoms and molecules form repeating patterns

CRYSTALLIZATION

the process resulting in the formation of crystals

ELEMENT

a substance found in nature that is in its simplest form

EMISSION

gas given off from a source—in this case, vehicles

ENCODE

convert into a code to save space

EVAPORATE

turn from liquid to gas or vapor

EXCAVATE

dig out

FLUORESCENT

absorbing light of one color and reflecting another, giving it the appearance of glowing

GEODE

a rock containing a cavity lined with minerals, sometimes in the form of gems

GEOLOGIST

an expert in the study of Earth's makeup and physical history

GEOMETRIC

containing regular lines and shapes

IGNEOUS

rock formed from cooled magma or lava

INORGANIC

not containing or coming from living things

LAPIDARY

someone who cuts and polishes gemstones

GLOSSARY

MAGMA

hot liquid found beneath Earth's crust

MICROSCOPIC

only seen using a microscope

MINERAL

a hard material from which rocks and gems are made that is found in nature and is not made of living things

MOLECULE

a group of atoms that join to form one unit

OPAQUE

not transparent

ORGANIC

containing or coming from living things

PIEZOELECTRIC EFFECT

electricity resulting from pressure

PREDATOR

an animal that hunts other animals for food

RADIATION

energy released through electromagnetic waves

RADIOACTIVE

releasing or containing radiation

SEDIMENTARY

rock that is formed by the deposition and subsequent cementation of that material at the earth's surface and within bodies of water

SYMMETRICAL

made of identical parts when facing each other

TECHNOLOGY

using science to improve day-to-day life

THEORY

an idea meant to explain something

THREE-DIMENSIONAL

having length, breadth, and depth

TRANSLUCENT

cloudy but allowing light to pass through

TRANSPARENT

clear and allowing light to pass through so things behind the transparent object can be seen clearly

Written by C.J. McDonald
Designed by Kat Peruyera

an imprint of

SCHOLASTIC
scholastic.com

10 9 8 7 6 5 4 3 2 1

ISBN: 978-1-338-34464-6

Printed in Guangzhou, China

Scholastic Inc., New York, NY

Cover design: Ali Castro
Photo research: Emily Teresa